AI in HR
A Blueprint for the Future

Actionable Insights for Seamless AI Integration in HR

CHIRAG KANSARA

To all the dedicated HR professionals around the world,

This book is for you—the tireless champions of talent, the stewards of organisational culture, and the unsung heroes who navigate the complexities of human resources with grace and resilience. Your commitment to fostering inclusive, ethical, and forward-thinking workplaces inspires us daily. May this book serve as a guide and a beacon as you embrace AI's transformative power, helping you enhance your invaluable work and lead your organisations into a bright, innovative future.

With gratitude and admiration,

Chirag Kansara

Contents

Foreword

The dawn of artificial intelligence (AI) has brought unprecedented changes across industries, and Human Resources (HR) is no exception. As we stand at the crossroads of technology and human potential, it becomes imperative to understand how AI can be harnessed to transform HR processes, enhance decision-making, and create more equitable workplaces.

This book, " AI in HR—A Blueprint for the Future," comes at a pivotal moment. It comprehensively explores how AI can be integrated into HR functions to drive efficiency, improve employee experiences, and foster a culture of innovation. But beyond the technological aspects, this book delves into ethical considerations and the need for responsible AI use—a crucial component in building trust and ensuring fair practices.

As an HR Tech professional with years of experience navigating the ever-evolving landscape of talent management with tech, I have witnessed firsthand the challenges and opportunities that come with technological advancements. The insights provided in this book are not just theoretical but grounded in practical applications, making it an invaluable resource for HR practitioners at all levels.

This book outlines a clear, actionable roadmap from identifying the first AI use cases to managing the transition and measuring impact. It emphasises the importance of starting small, learning continuously, and scaling strategically. Each chapter builds on the last, providing a holistic view of AI integration that is both manageable and impactful.

This book will guide HR leaders, helping them navigate the complexities of AI implementation while staying true to the core values of empathy, fairness, and human-centric leadership. The future of HR is not about replacing humans with machines but about augmenting human capabilities with intelligent systems to unlock new levels of potential.

As you embark on this journey of discovery and innovation, may you find inspiration, practical guidance, and a renewed sense of purpose. The road ahead is filled with opportunities, and with the right approach, we can create more efficient, inclusive, and fulfilling workplaces.

Welcome to the future of HR.

Sincerely,

Chirag Kansara, Founder and CTO - AppliView Technologies| www.appliview.com | chirag@appliview.com

Prologue/Introduction

Imagine a workplace where technology seamlessly supports and enhances every aspect of human potential. A place where mundane tasks are automated, allowing HR professionals to focus on strategic initiatives and personal connections that drive organisational success. In this future vision, artificial intelligence (AI) is not just a tool but a trusted partner that helps unlock new levels of efficiency, fairness, and innovation.

This book is a journey into that future.

In the early days of HR, the focus was primarily on administrative tasks—managing payroll, handling employee records, and ensuring compliance with regulations. Over the years, the role of HR has evolved to become a strategic partner in shaping organisational culture, driving employee engagement, and fostering leadership development. Today, we stand on the brink of another significant transformation driven by AI.

AI promises to revolutionise HR in ways we are only beginning to understand. It has the potential to eliminate biases in hiring, provide personalised employee development plans, predict and mitigate turnover, and much more. However, with great power comes great responsibility. As we integrate AI into HR processes, we must remain vigilant about ethical considerations, data privacy, and the need for human oversight.

This book aims to bridge the gap between AI's potential and its practical application in HR. It offers a comprehensive guide to navigating this new landscape, providing insights, strategies, and best practices for leveraging AI to enhance rather than replace human capabilities.

Each chapter is designed to build upon the previous one, guiding you through the complexities of AI integration—from identifying the first use case to scaling AI across the organisation. We explore the ethical implications, discuss regulatory frameworks, and offer practical steps for ensuring continuous improvement and alignment with organisational goals.

You will find a blend of visionary thinking and practical advice as you read through these pages. The future of HR is not about choosing between technology and people; it's about finding the right balance that allows both to thrive. By embracing AI thoughtfully and responsibly, we can create more efficient and human workplaces.

Welcome to a journey of discovery, innovation, and transformation. The future of HR is here, filled with exciting possibilities.

Let's explore them together.

Chirag Kansara

The Future Landscape of AI in HR

2030 Vision: AI Transforms HR at TechSolutions Inc

A Day in the Life of HR at TechSolutions Inc.

It's 2030, and the global corporation TechSolutions Inc. is at the forefront of innovation. Inside its bustling headquarters, the Human Resources (HR) department hums with activity, but there's something distinctly different about it. Unlike the HR departments of the past, nearly every task here is seamlessly managed by advanced artificial intelligence (AI) systems. From recruitment to employee engagement, AI has redefined how HR operates, making processes faster, more efficient, and more inclusive.

Good morning at TechSolutions Inc.: Meet Alex, the chief HR officer at TechSolutions Inc. As Alex walks into the office at 9 AM, she is greeted by an AI-powered virtual assistant named Eva. Eva provides personalised updates on Alex's schedule, meetings, and tasks for the day. New hires like Sam, a software engineer, are welcomed by AI-driven onboarding programs that tailor their experience based on individual roles and preferences.

Automated Recruitment with TalentScout AI: In the recruitment corner, meet Lisa, an HR specialist who relies on an AI system called TalentScout AI to handle job applications that have poured in overnight. TalentScout AI uses sophisticated algorithms to screen resumes, evaluating candidates' skills, experiences, and cultural fit. By 10 AM, TalentScout AI has already shortlisted the top candidates, scheduled interviews, and sent personalised messages to each applicant. It even provides Lisa with insights on how each candidate matches the job requirements, reducing the risk of bias and improving the quality of hires.

Employee Engagement with EngageBot: Across the office, EngageBot, an AI tool, monitors employee sentiment in real-time, analysing feedback from digital surveys, emails, and even casual conversations captured through communication platforms. EngageBot identifies trends, highlights potential areas of concern, and suggests actionable insights to improve workplace morale. For instance, David, a project manager, receives a notification about an upcoming team-building activity designed to boost morale based on recent feedback.

Performance Management with PerformancePlus AI: In the performance management section, AI systems like PerformancePlus AI provide continuous feedback to employees like Maria, a marketing executive. PerformancePlus AI tracks performance metrics, recognises achievements, and offers personalised development plans. Maria receives notifications about her progress and suggestions for training programs tailored to her career goals. The system also predicts potential career paths for Maria based on her performance and interests, helping her plan her future within the company.

Learning and Development with LearnMate AI: AI-powered learning platforms like LearnMate AI recommend courses and training sessions based on individual career paths. These platforms use machine learning to adapt content to each employee's learning style and pace, ensuring everyone gets the most out of their training. For instance, Raj, a junior data analyst, is recommended a series of courses to enhance his data visualisation skills. LearnMate AI also tracks the effectiveness of these courses and adjusts future recommendations accordingly.

Employee Wellness with WellBeing AI: By midday, WellBeing AI systems are already identifying potential wellness issues. They monitor physical and mental health indicators, providing personalised wellness tips and scheduling activities that promote well-being. Employees like

Sarah, who has been feeling stressed, can interact with WellBeing AI-driven wellness coaches to discuss their health and receive tailored advice. The system even integrates with wearable devices to monitor physical activity and suggest improvements.

Strategic Workforce Planning with WorkforceWizard AI: WorkforceWizard AI tools forecast future workforce needs in the strategic planning room. They analyse market trends, predict skill shortages, and suggest talent acquisition and retention strategies. HR professionals use these insights to make informed decisions that align with the company's long-term goals. Alex, the Chief HR Officer, reviews these insights to ensure TechSolutions Inc. is prepared for future challenges. WorkforceWizard AI also simulates different scenarios, helping Alex develop contingency plans.

Transition to Real-World Integration

While TechSolutions Inc.'s scenario is a work of fiction set in the future, the journey toward an AI-integrated HR department has already begun. Companies worldwide are experimenting with and implementing AI technologies in their HR processes. The tools and systems that make TechSolutions Inc. so efficient are inspired by genuine innovations today.

The Rise of AI in Industries

AI is no longer futuristic; it's making waves across various sectors. From healthcare to finance, AI is driving innovations once thought impossible. AI algorithms analyse patient data in healthcare to predict diseases and recommend treatments. In finance, AI systems detect fraudulent transactions and optimise investment strategies. These examples highlight AI's potential to revolutionise traditional practices and bring about significant improvements.

AI in the HR Landscape

The integration of AI is profoundly transforming the HR landscape. HR professionals leverage AI tools to automate repetitive tasks, analyse vast amounts of data, and make data-driven decisions. This transformation is not just about efficiency; it's about enhancing the employee experience and fostering a more inclusive and productive work environment.

Here are a few ways AI is being used in HR:

1. **Automated Recruitment:** AI-powered systems streamline recruitment by automating resume screening, scheduling interviews, and conducting initial assessments through chatbots.

2. **Employee Engagement:** AI tools analyse employee feedback and sentiment, providing insights that help HR teams address concerns and improve workplace morale.

3. **Learning and Development:** AI identifies skill gaps and recommends personalised training programs, ensuring employees have the necessary resources to grow.

Key Players in AI-Driven HR

Several key players are driving the AI revolution in HR. Tech giants like Google, IBM, and Microsoft are developing advanced AI tools tailored for HR functions. Startups are also entering the market with innovative solutions that address specific HR challenges, from bias-free recruitment to real-time employee feedback.

Example: A company named AppliView uses AI to analyse video interviews. Their system assesses candidates' facial expressions, word choices, and speaking patterns to provide insights into their suitability for a role. This technology aims to reduce human bias and improve the fairness of hiring decisions.

The Initial Integration of AI Technologies

The initial integration of AI technologies into HR processes was met with excitement and scepticism. Companies saw the potential for increased efficiency and better decision-making, but there were concerns about data privacy, ethical considerations, and the potential displacement of HR jobs.

To address these concerns, organisations started small, implementing AI in specific areas like recruitment and employee engagement. Over time, as the benefits became evident, the adoption of AI in HR expanded. Early adopters shared success stories, demonstrating how AI could lead to better hiring outcomes, improved employee satisfaction, and more strategic HR planning.

Benefits of AI in HR

The benefits of integrating AI into HR are vast:

1. **Efficiency:** AI automates repetitive tasks, freeing HR professionals to focus on strategic initiatives.

2. **Data-Driven Decisions:** AI analyses large datasets to provide actionable insights, helping HR teams make informed decisions.

3. **Bias Reduction:** AI can help reduce unconscious bias in hiring and promotions, promoting a more diverse and inclusive workplace.

Challenges of Integrating AI in HR

While the benefits are significant, integrating AI into HR also presents challenges:

1. **Bias in AI Algorithms:** AI systems can perpetuate existing biases if not carefully designed. Ensuring fairness and transparency in AI algorithms is crucial.

2. **Privacy Concerns:** Protecting employee data is paramount. Organisations must implement robust data security measures to maintain trust.

3. **Change Management:** Introducing AI requires a cultural shift. HR teams need to be trained and comfortable working alongside AI tools.

The dawn of AI in HR marks the beginning of an exciting journey. In the following chapters, we will explore the various aspects of AI-driven HR and see how these intelligent systems transform HR processes and enhance employees' overall work experience.

In the next chapter, we'll explore AI's revolutionary changes to recruitment, precisely how they eliminate human selection bias and ensure fairer hiring practices. Join us as we uncover the next step in this fascinating evolution.

2. Mindset Matters: Paving the Way for AI Integration

"The mind is everything. What you think, you become." – Buddha.

The previous chapter explored a futuristic vision of how AI transforms HR at TechSolutions Inc. It's 2030, and nearly every HR task is managed by advanced AI systems, creating an efficient and inclusive workplace. This seamless integration of AI has made processes faster and more personalised, significantly altering the HR landscape. However, a crucial change is needed to reach this level of innovation: a shift in mindset.

Adopting AI is not just about integrating new technologies into existing workflows; it requires a fundamental change in how we perceive and approach work. In this chapter, we will explore the importance of developing an "AI mindset" and how it serves as the foundation for successful AI adoption. We'll discuss why changing our mindset is the first step towards leveraging AI's full potential and transforming our approach to skills, experience, and the future of work.

The Safety-First Mindset for AI.

Almost 25 years ago, during my industrial safety training, I emphasised that safety isn't just a protocol—it's a mindset. This mindset was crucial because it wasn't just about following rules but ingraining a culture where safety was second nature. Fast forward to the present, and I see AI in the same light. Without the right mindset, diving into AI is like trying to swim without water. It's foundational, not a quick fix when trouble strikes.

When approaching AI, we need to adopt a "safety-first mindset." This means prioritising ethical considerations, data privacy, and the potential impacts on society. It's about being proactive rather than reactive, ensuring that AI systems are designed and deployed with caution and foresight.

The Productivity Myth: AI is Not a Magical Solution

Let's get real: AI isn't a magic solution for every productivity challenge we face. It's about betterment, handling repetitive tasks, and enabling more intelligent analysis. AI helps make decisions and execute tasks but won't brew your morning coffee. Instead, it offers a leap in how we approach work.

For example, in customer service, AI can handle routine inquiries, allowing human agents to focus on complex issues requiring empathy and nuanced understanding. AI can analyse vast financial datasets to provide investment insights, but the final decision still benefits from human judgment.

Adopting AI starts with changing our mindset. We must understand that AI is a powerful tool to enhance our capabilities, not replace them. This shift in perspective is crucial for effectively integrating AI into our work processes.

The Reality of Job Replacement: Adapt or Be Left Behind

Imagine a world where AI does all our work, rendering the idea of 'hard work' obsolete. It sounds like a utopian dream, but it could quickly become a nightmare for those who don't adapt. If AI could handle 'all' our tasks, it would immediately replace those who do not use it.

The future with AI will not entirely replace jobs but will favour those who've embraced and mastered its use over those who've kept it at arm's length. The stark reality? It's not jobs that are at risk; it's the people unwilling to adapt to using AI effectively who might find themselves sidelined.

For instance, marketing analysts who leverage AI to enhance their insights and strategies will outperform those who don't. AI can analyse consumer behaviour and predict trends more quickly and accurately than humans. A mindset that welcomes and integrates AI into daily tasks is critical to thriving in this new landscape.

Early Adoption: The Need for a Proactive Mindset

Are you considering waiting until AI is "cool," when your colleague starts using it, or when your company gets all the required tools? Think again. AI's evolution is racing at the speed of light. Waiting until it's fully mature means missing out on growing alongside it.

Businesses that adopted AI early in their operations have gained a significant competitive edge. They can process more data, respond to market changes faster, and innovate more effectively. Similarly, professionals who learn to use AI early will find themselves at the forefront of their fields.

To truly benefit from AI, we must change our mindset from passive acceptance to proactive learning and integration. This means staying curious, continuously learning, and not being afraid to experiment with AI tools.

AI as a Transformative Partner

Embracing AI requires us to see it not as a threat but as a dynamic partner. AI is like our dynamic twin, evolving alongside us—ready to learn, grow, and embark on life's adventures together. This shift in mindset is essential for navigating the future of work powered by AI.

We're talking about a quantum leap in approaching work powered by AI. It's not magic, but it's undeniably transformative. By adopting the right mindset, we can ensure that AI becomes a valuable tool that enhances our skills, productivity, and overall job satisfaction.

Adopting the right mindset is crucial for effective AI integration. By embracing a proactive and safety-first approach, organisations can ensure AI becomes a valuable tool that enhances productivity and job satisfaction.

The next chapter will explore how AI is revolutionising job market equalisation, breaking down barriers, and empowering underrepresented groups. Join us as we delve into the transformative potential of AI in creating a more equitable job marke

3. AI and Job Market Equalization

Levelling the Playing Field: AI's Role in Job Market Equality

In the first chapter, we painted a picture of how HR might look at TechSolutions Inc. We saw how AI tools handle various HR tasks, making processes more efficient and fair. Now, let's dive deeper into one of the most significant benefits of AI in HR: job market equalisation. This means giving everyone an equal chance to get a job, regardless of their background.

Breaking Down Barriers

In the traditional job market, various biases can affect hiring decisions. These biases can be based on a person's gender, race, age, or even the school they attended. AI has the potential to minimise these biases. Here's how:

1. **Blind Recruitment:**

   - **How it works:** AI systems, like TalentScout (a hypothetical future AI) used at TechSolutions Inc., remove personal information such as names, photos, and addresses from resumes. This process, known as blind recruitment, helps ensure that candidates are evaluated based on their skills and experience alone.

   - **Impact:** This method reduces the chances of unconscious bias affecting hiring decisions. For instance, Lisa, our HR specialist from the first chapter, uses TalentScout AI to review resumes without knowing the candidates' details, making her assessments fairer.

1. **Standardised Assessments:**

   o **How it works:** AI-driven tools, like ChatHire, conduct initial assessments and interviews. These tools ask the same questions to all candidates and evaluate responses based on predefined criteria.

   o **Impact:** Standardized assessments ensure that all candidates are judged on the same criteria, reducing the influence of subjective opinions. This helps in selecting the best candidate for the job based on merit.

   o

2. **Diverse Candidate Sourcing:**

   o **How it works:** AI can search for candidates from various sources, including online job boards, social media, and professional networks. Tools like DiverseTalent AI focus on sourcing candidates from underrepresented groups.

   o **Impact:** By broadening the search, AI helps companies find qualified candidates they might have overlooked, increasing organisational diversity.

Empowering Underrepresented Groups

AI removes biases and empowers those traditionally excluded from the job market.

1. **Accessibility:**

   o **How it works:** AI tools can be designed to be accessible to people with disabilities. For example, AccessibleHire AI provides voice-controlled applications and assessments for visually impaired candidates.

   o **Impact:** These tools ensure that candidates with disabilities have equal opportunities to apply for and secure jobs. They make the hiring process more inclusive and accessible to everyone.

2. **Skill Development:**

   o **How it works:** AI can identify skill gaps and recommend training programs. Platforms like SkillBoost AI analyse individuals' skills and suggest relevant courses to improve their employability.

   o **Impact:** By providing personalised learning paths, AI helps people develop the skills they need to compete in the job market. This is especially beneficial for individuals from disadvantaged backgrounds who may have yet to access quality education.

AI holds great promise in creating a more equal job market by reducing biases and providing opportunities for underrepresented groups. However, careful implementation and ongoing oversight are essential to ensure these tools are used ethically and effectively.

In the next chapter, we will examine how AI is transforming jobs requiring high analytical skills and the implications for the workforce. Join us as we delve into the disruption of analytical jobs and explore what this means for the future.

4. The Disruption of Analytical Jobs

Redefining Experience and Skill: AI's Impact on High-Skill and Knowledge-Based Jobs

In previous chapters, we explored how AI can create a more equal job market and the ethical considerations involved. Now, let's delve into how AI is redefining jobs that require high skill and experience, particularly in fields that rely heavily on knowledge and analytical expertise.

The Transformation of Experience and Skill

AI is set to revolutionise the traditional concepts of experience and skill. Future AI systems will embody the collective experience and knowledge humanity has accumulated on any subject. This transformation means that a person at the age of 20, equipped with AI tools, could perform tasks with the efficiency and expertise of someone with 30 years of experience. This is especially true for professions that rely on computer-based work or knowledge and experience, such as consultancy services.

For roles requiring fieldwork or hands-on interaction with machinery, humans will continue to hold the reins for the foreseeable future. However, even these areas will eventually shift as robotics and AI technology advance.

AI's Re-Definition of Knowledge

Today's understanding of knowledge as something we perceive or collect is set to change dramatically with AI. AI will shift from gathering information to generating and processing it instantaneously, making real-time insights and decisions based on vast datasets and historical trends.

Automation of Analytical Tasks

AI systems, particularly those powered by advanced machine learning, can automate numerous analytical tasks that previously required human expertise:

- **Data Analysis**: AI can rapidly analyse large datasets, uncovering patterns and insights far more quickly than humans.

- **Pattern Recognition**: AI excels at identifying trends and anomalies that might elude human analysts.

- **Forecasting**: AI can make precise predictions based on historical data.

- **Decision-Making**: AI provides data-driven recommendations, aiding in complex decision-making processes.

As a result, some traditional analytical roles may become redundant, prompting professionals in these fields to shift their focus or adapt their responsibilities.

Augmentation of Human Capabilities

While AI can automate specific tasks, it also enhances human capabilities in various ways:

- **Data Processing**: AI's ability to handle vast amounts of data allows analysts to work more efficiently.

- **Identifying Patterns**: AI can reveal connections in data that humans might not easily see.

- **Providing Insights**: AI generates insights that enable analysts to make better-informed decisions.

This augmentation improves the productivity and decision-making abilities of analysts, researchers, and other professionals who work with complex data.

Demand for New Skills (More in Next Chapter)

As AI transforms the nature of analytical work, new skills will become essential:

- **AI Development**: Professionals who can develop and maintain AI systems will be in high demand.

- **Data Engineering**: Managing and engineering large datasets will become increasingly valuable.

- **AI Ethics**: Understanding the ethical implications of AI will be crucial.

Workers must adapt by acquiring these new skills to remain relevant in the evolving job market.

Shift in Job Roles and Responsibilities

The integration of AI will lead to significant changes in job roles and responsibilities:

- **Obsolete Roles**: Some traditional analytical roles may need to be updated.

- **New Roles**: Job titles like AI model developers, data engineers, and AI ethics specialists will emerge.

- **Adapting Roles**: Existing professionals may need to adjust their skills and responsibilities to work alongside AI. For example, a financial analyst might use AI tools to gather insights instead of manually analysing data, allowing them to focus on strategic decision-making.

Navigating the Changes

To navigate these changes, organisations and individuals must:

- **Lifelong Learning**: Embrace continuous learning to stay updated with new skills.

- **Reskilling Initiatives**: Invest in programs to help workers develop new skills.

- **Human-AI Collaboration**: Foster a culture where humans and AI systems work together effectively.

AI is redefining the concepts of experience and skill, especially in fields that rely on analytical and knowledge-based tasks. AI transforms the workforce by automating repetitive tasks, augmenting human capabilities, and creating new job roles. While this shift brings numerous benefits, it also presents challenges that must be navigated with continuous learning, reskilling initiatives, and a strong emphasis on ethical considerations.

In the next chapter, we will delve into the new job opportunities created by AI. As AI systems become more widespread, they necessitate creating new roles and evolving existing ones. Join us as we explore the emerging careers in the AI era, the synergy between humans and AI, and the crucial importance of reskilling and upskilling to stay relevant in this rapidly evolving landscape.

5. New Job Opportunities Created by AI

Building the Future: New Careers in the AI Era

In the previous chapter, we discussed how AI is transforming analytical jobs. Now, let's explore the new job opportunities created by AI. As AI systems become more common, they demand new roles and the evolution of existing ones. This chapter will cover the various new job roles emerging due to AI, the collaboration between humans and AI, and the importance of reskilling and upskilling.

AI Development and Implementation

As AI becomes widespread, there is a growing need for professionals who can create and maintain these systems. Here are some key roles:

1. **AI/Machine Learning Engineers:**
   - **Role:** Design, build, and optimise AI models and algorithms.
   - **Skills Needed:** Coding, knowledge of machine learning frameworks, and problem-solving abilities.
2. **Data Scientists/Engineers:**
   - **Role:** Collect, process, and prepare data for AI systems.
   - **Skills Needed:** Data analysis, statistical knowledge, and programming skills.
3. **AI Ethics Specialists:**
   - **Role:** Ensure AI systems are ethical and responsible, addressing issues like bias and privacy.
   - **Skills Needed:** Understanding of AI, ethics, and legal standards.

AI-Human Collaboration

While AI can automate specific tasks, many jobs involve human collaboration and AI systems. This creates new roles focused on leveraging AI capabilities:

1. **AI Trainers:**

   - o **Role:** Curate and label data to train AI models and monitor their performance.
   - o **Skills Needed:** Attention to detail, understanding of AI models, and data management.

2. **AI Explainers:**

   - o **Role:** Interpret and communicate the insights and decisions generated by AI systems to stakeholders.
   - o **Skills Needed:** Communication skills, understanding of AI, and data interpretation.

3. **AI Interaction Designers:**

   - o **Role:** Develop user interfaces and experiences for seamless human-AI collaboration.
   - o **Skills Needed:** Design skills, user experience (UX) knowledge, and understanding of AI.

AI-Enabled Roles

AI can augment and enhance existing roles, creating new opportunities for specialised skills:

1. **AI-Assisted Professionals:**
   - o **Examples:** Doctors, lawyers, and financial analysts.
   - o **Impact:** Use AI to analyse data, identify patterns, and generate insights, allowing them to focus on higher-level tasks.
2. **AI Content Creators:**
   - o **Examples:** Writers, artists, and designers.
   - o **Impact:** Use AI tools to generate ideas, enhance creativity, and streamline content production.
3. **AI Strategists:**
   - o **Role:** Develop strategies for integrating AI into business processes, products, and services to drive innovation and growth.

- o **Skills Needed:** Strategic thinking, understanding of AI, and business acumen.

Reskilling and Upskilling

As AI automates specific tasks, there will be a need for reskilling and upskilling programs to help workers transition to new roles and acquire the necessary skills for an AI-driven workforce:

1. **AI Education and Training:**
   - o **Focus:** Teaching technical skills like coding and data analysis.
2. **Career Counselling and Workforce Development:**
   - o **Focus:** Helping individuals identify new career paths and necessary training.
3. **Lifelong Learning Initiatives:**
   - o **Focus:** Encouraging continuous learning to adapt to changing job requirements.

The Future of Work with AI

The future of AI work will require a combination of technical skills and human skills that are difficult to automate. These include:

1. **Technical Skills:**
   - o Coding, data analysis, and understanding of AI technologies.
2. **Human Skills:**
   - o Critical thinking, creativity, and emotional intelligence.

AI is creating a wealth of new job opportunities and transforming existing roles. While it presents challenges, it also offers immense potential for growth and innovation.

In the next chapter, we will delve into the ethical considerations of AI in HR. Join us as we explore the challenges and solutions to ensuring fair, transparent, and accountable AI use in the workplace.

.

6. The Ethics of AI in HR

Ethical Boundaries: Navigating AI in HR

In the last chapter, we explored how AI can help create a more equal and new job market by reducing biases and providing opportunities for underrepresented groups. However, as with any powerful tool, AI in HR has ethical considerations that we must carefully navigate. This chapter will discuss the moral issues surrounding AI in HR and how to address them.

Understanding Ethical Issues

When we talk about ethics in AI, we refer to the principles that guide the fair and just use of technology. Here are some critical ethical issues that arise when using AI in HR:

Bias and Discrimination

One significant ethical risk is the potential for AI systems to perpetuate or amplify existing biases and discrimination in hiring, performance evaluation, and other HR processes.

AI models can inadvertently learn and reinforce biases in the training data, leading to unfair and discriminatory outcomes. For example, an AI resume screening tool trained on historical data favouring specific demographics may systematically disadvantage candidates from underrepresented groups.

Addressing Bias in AI

Bias in AI can have serious consequences, but there are ways to mitigate it:

1. **Diverse Data Sets:**

   o **What to do:** Use diverse and representative data sets to train AI systems. This helps ensure the AI makes fair decisions.

   o **Example:** Including data from various demographic groups when training an AI hiring tool.

2. **Regular Audits:**

   o **What to do:** Conduct regular audits of AI systems to check for and correct biases.

   o **Example:** Periodically reviewing AI hiring decisions to ensure they are fair and unbiased.

3. **Inclusive Teams:**

   o **What to do:** Have diverse teams develop and oversee AI systems. Different perspectives can help identify and reduce biases.

   o **Example:** Involving team members from different backgrounds in developing an AI tool.

Privacy and Data Protection

AI systems in HR often rely on collecting and analysing vast amounts of personal data about employees, such as performance metrics, communication patterns, and even biometric data. This raises significant privacy concerns and potential misuse or unauthorised access to sensitive information. Organisations must implement robust data protection measures and obtain informed consent from employees.

Protecting Privacy

Protecting the privacy of candidates and employees is crucial:

1. **Data Protection Policies:**

   o **What to do:** Implement robust data protection policies and ensure regulation compliance.

   o **Example:** Following GDPR guidelines to protect personal data in the EU.

2. **Secure Data Storage:**

   o **What to do:** Use secure methods to store and handle data.

   o **Example:** Encrypting data and limiting access to authorised personnel only.

Transparency and Explainability

Many AI systems, particularly those using machine learning, operate as "black boxes," making it difficult to understand how decisions are made. This lack of transparency and explainability can undermine trust in HR processes and raise concerns about fairness and accountability. Organisations should strive to make AI decision-making processes as transparent and explainable as possible.

Ensuring Transparency

Transparency in AI is essential for building trust:

1. **Explainable AI:**

   o **What to do:** Use AI systems that explain their decisions.

   o **Example:** An AI tool that provides reasons for rejecting a job application.

2. **Clear Communication:**

   o **What to do:** Communicate clearly with candidates and employees about how AI is used in HR processes.

- o **Example:** Inform job applicants that AI will be used to screen their resumes and explain how it works.

Human Oversight and Control

More reliance on AI could dehumanise HR processes and lead to loss of human oversight and control. While AI can assist in streamlining tasks, it is crucial to maintain human involvement in decision-making, particularly in sensitive areas like hiring and performance evaluation.

Maintaining Human Oversight

Even with AI, human oversight is essential:

1. **Human Oversight:**

   - o **What to do:** Ensure that human HR professionals oversee AI decisions.

   - o **Example:** Having an HR manager review AI-generated shortlists of job candidates.

2. **Clear Responsibility:**

   - o **What to do:** Establish clear lines of responsibility for AI systems.

   - o **Example:** Assigning a specific team to monitor and manage AI tools.

Balancing Efficiency and Fairness

While AI promises to increase efficiency in HR processes, this should not come at the expense of fairness and ethical considerations. Organisations must balance leveraging AI's benefits and ensuring its use does not compromise ethical principles or employee well-being.

Striking the Right Balance

1. **Ethical AI Policies:**

   o **What to do:** Establish clear AI ethics policies.

   o **Example:** Creating guidelines that prioritise fairness and non-discrimination in AI applications.

2. **Involving Stakeholders:**

   o **What to do:** Involve employees and stakeholders in decision-making processes related to AI.

   o **Example:** Holding workshops and consultations to gather input on AI use in HR.

Ethical considerations are crucial when using AI in HR. We can ensure that AI is used responsibly and ethically by addressing issues like bias, transparency, privacy, and accountability.

In the next chapter, we will explore the potential risks of over-relying on AI, including the possibility of job market collapse.

.

7. The Potential for Job Market Collapse

A World Without Jobs? The Risks of Over-Reliance on AI

In the previous chapters, we explored the new job opportunities AI creates and how it transforms the workforce. But what if AI were to replace most traditional jobs? This scenario could have far-reaching societal impacts that need to be carefully managed.

Let's explore the potential risks and implications of a job market heavily influenced by AI automation.

Economic Disruption

If AI were to replace many traditional jobs, it could lead to significant economic disruption.

1. **Mass Unemployment and Income Inequality:**

   - **Impact:** Large segments of the workforce might be displaced by AI automation across various industries, leading to mass unemployment and increasing income inequality. This could result in social unrest and economic instability as people struggle to find new employment opportunities.

   - **Example:** Industries like manufacturing, transportation, and even some services could see widespread job losses as AI systems become capable of performing tasks more efficiently than humans.

2. **Shift in Wealth and Power:**

   - o **Impact:** Those controlling AI technologies and capital could accumulate disproportionate gains, while others face job losses. This could widen the gap between the wealthy and the poor, concentrating wealth and power in the hands of a few.

   - o **Example:** Tech companies that develop and deploy AI systems might see massive profits while traditional businesses and workers suffer.

Social Implications

The societal impacts of widespread AI adoption go beyond economic disruption.

1. **Loss of Purpose and Identity:**

   - o **Impact:** Many individuals derive their sense of self-worth and social status from their jobs. Losing employment could lead to a loss of purpose and identity, affecting their mental and emotional well-being.

   - o **Example:** A factory worker who has spent decades mastering their craft might struggle to find meaning in a world where their job no longer exists.

2. **Mental Health Issues:**

   - o **Impact:** Job insecurity and lack of meaningful work could lead to an increase in mental health issues like depression and anxiety. People might feel hopeless and disconnected from society.

- o **Example:** Communities with high unemployment rates often see higher incidences of mental health problems.

  o

3. **Disruption of Family Structures and Gender Roles:**

   - o **Impact:** Traditional family structures and gender roles might be disrupted as breadwinners lose employment. This could change dynamics within households and create additional stress.

   - o **Example:** A shift in employment patterns could lead to more women entering the workforce or more men staying home, challenging traditional gender roles.

Education and Skill Development

To cope with the changes brought by AI, education systems need to evolve.

1. **Revamping Education Systems:**

   - o **Need:** Education systems must focus on skills that complement AI, such as creativity, emotional intelligence, and critical thinking, rather than competing.

   - o **Example:** Schools might emphasise the arts, humanities, and social sciences alongside STEM (Science, Technology, Engineering, and Mathematics) subjects to prepare students for a future where human skills are valued.

2. **Retraining and Upskilling Initiatives:**

   o **Need:** Displaced workers will need massive retraining and upskilling to transition into new roles and industries.

   o **Example:** Governments and businesses could invest in training programs to help workers learn new skills relevant to the AI-driven job market.

Ethical and Philosophical Considerations

The rise of AI in the workforce raises profound ethical and philosophical questions.

1. **Moral and Ethical Implications:**

   o **Questions:** Is allowing AI to replace human labour on a large scale right? What are the dehumanising effects of this transition?

   o **Example:** Debates might arise about the role of work in human life and the ethics of replacing jobs with machines.

2. **Purpose of Work and Distribution of Wealth:**

   o **Debates:** Society must reconsider the purpose of work and how wealth and resources are distributed in an AI-driven economy.

   o **Example:** Discussions around implementing universal basic income or job guarantees to ensure everyone has a means of support.

Governance and Policy Challenges

Effective governance and policy-making will be crucial in transitioning to an AI-driven economy.

1. **Support for Displaced Workers:**

   o **Need:** Governments might need to implement policies and social safety nets, such as universal basic income or job guarantees, to support displaced workers and mitigate economic disruption.

   o **Example:** Pilot programs for universal basic income in various countries could provide a model for broader implementation.

2. **Regulatory Frameworks:**

   o **Need:** New regulatory frameworks will be necessary to govern the development and deployment of AI technologies, ensuring accountability, transparency, and ethical use.

   o **Example:** Regulations could mandate regular audits of AI systems to check for biases and ensure fair use.

Proactive Measures for a Smooth Transition

A coordinated effort involving policymakers, businesses, educators, and civil society will be crucial to navigating such a profound societal shift. Here are some proactive measures:

1. **Investing in Education:**

   o **Action:** Invest in education systems that emphasise technical and human skills to prepare students for a future with AI.

2. **Fostering Public-Private Partnerships:**

   o **Action:** Encourage collaboration between governments and businesses to develop training programs and create new job opportunities.

3. **Exploring New Economic Models:**

   o **Action:** Consider new economic models, like universal basic income, to ensure a fair distribution of wealth and resources.

The potential for AI to replace traditional jobs poses significant risks and challenges. However, with careful planning, proactive measures, and a commitment to ethical practices, we can navigate these changes and create a future where AI benefits everyone.

In the next chapter, we will discuss AI's global impact on HR and how different regions adapt to these changes. Join us as we explore AI's worldwide implications for HR.

.

8. The Global Impact of AI on HR

Beyond Borders: How AI is Transforming HR Worldwide

Adopting AI in HR is a global phenomenon, with organisations across different regions and cultures embracing this transformative technology. While the specific applications and challenges may vary, several common trends are emerging worldwide.

Let's explore how AI shapes HR practices worldwide, particularly in facilitating global, cross-cultural, and cross-regional operations.

Automating Repetitive Tasks

One of the primary drivers for AI adoption in HR is the automation of repetitive and time-consuming tasks. This is particularly beneficial for global organisations that operate across multiple regions:

1. **Resume Screening:**

    - **How it works:** AI-powered tools can quickly sift through hundreds of resumes, identifying the most qualified candidates based on predefined criteria, regardless of location.

    - **Impact:** This reduces the workload on HR professionals globally, allowing them to focus on more strategic activities and ensure a standardised approach to candidate evaluation across different regions

2. **Candidate Sourcing:**

    - **How it works:** AI systems can scan online job boards, social media, and professional networks worldwide to find potential candidates.

- o **Impact:** This helps organisations build a diverse global talent pool more efficiently, ensuring they reach the best candidates from different regions and cultures.

3. **Employee Data Management:**

   - o **How it works:** AI automates the management of employee records, performance data, and other HR-related information across multiple regions.

   - o **Impact:** This ensures data accuracy and consistency, facilitating smoother operations in multinational organisations.

4. **Payroll Processing:**

   - o **How it works:** AI systems handle payroll calculations, tax deductions, and benefits administration across different countries with varying regulations.

   - o **Impact:** This reduces errors and ensures timely employee payment worldwide, accommodating regional laws and standards.

Enhancing Talent Acquisition

AI is revolutionising talent acquisition by enabling more efficient and data-driven recruitment processes, which is crucial for global organisations:

1. **Analysing Candidate Data:**

   - o **How it works:** AI tools analyse vast amounts of candidate data from around the world, including resumes, social media profiles, and past job performance.

   - o **Impact:** This helps identify top talent quickly and accurately, regardless of their geographic location, and ensures a diverse hiring process.

2. **Matching Candidates with Roles:**

   o **How it works:** AI matches candidates to suitable roles based on their skills, experience, and cultural fit, considering regional differences.

   o **Impact:** This improves the quality of hires and reduces turnover rates, ensuring that the best candidates are selected for roles in different parts of the world.

3. **Global Recruitment:**

   o **How it works:** AI tools facilitate global recruitment by managing different time zones, languages, and legal requirements.

   o **Impact:** This is particularly valuable for multinational organisations seeking to attract and retain a diverse workforce, as it ensures that recruitment processes are efficient and culturally sensitive.

Mitigating Bias and Discrimination

AI can help mitigate bias and discrimination in HR processes, which is critical for global companies:

1. **Objective Evaluation:**

   o **How it works:** AI algorithms, when trained on diverse and representative data, evaluate candidates and employees based on their qualifications and performance, not personal characteristics.

   o **Impact:** This helps create a fairer hiring process, reduce unconscious biases' effects, and promote workplace diversity across different regions.

2. **Cultural Sensitivity:**

- o **How it works:** AI systems can be programmed to understand and respect cultural differences, ensuring that recruitment and HR practices are inclusive.

- o **Impact:** This helps multinational companies maintain a respectful and inclusive workplace culture, accommodating various cultural norms and values.

Personalised Employee Experiences

AI enables organisations to provide more personalised experiences for their employees, which is crucial in a global context:

1. **Tailored Learning and Development:**

   - o **How it works:** AI analyses employee preferences, behaviours, and performance data to recommend tailored learning and development opportunities.

   - o **Impact:** This ensures that employees from different regions receive relevant training that meets their needs and career goals.

2. **Customised Benefits Packages:**

   - o **How it works:** AI can design personalised benefits packages that cater to the diverse needs of a global workforce.

   - o **Impact:** This enhances employee satisfaction and retention, as employees feel valued and supported regardless of location.

3. **Personalised Career Paths:**

   - o **How it works:** AI systems can map customised career paths based on individual aspirations and regional opportunities.

- o **Impact:** This helps employees see a clear path for growth within the company, increasing motivation and engagement.

Cultural and Regulatory Challenges

While AI offers numerous benefits, its adoption in HR is not without challenges, especially on a global scale:

1. **Navigating Cultural Differences:**

   - o **Challenge:** Different regions have different cultural norms and values that must be respected.

   - o **Solution:** AI systems must be designed with cultural sensitivity, ensuring they respect and accommodate these differences.

2. **Regulatory Landscapes:**

   - o **Challenge:** Different countries have varying laws and regulations regarding data privacy and employment.

   - o **Solution:** Organizations must ensure compliance with local laws and regulations, and AI systems must be flexible enough to adapt to these legal requirements.

3. **Gaining Employee Trust:**

   - o **Challenge:** Employees may be sceptical of AI systems and concerned about privacy and fairness.

   - o **Solution:** Transparency and clear communication about AI can help build trust. Ensuring ethical AI practices and demonstrating the benefits of AI can also alleviate concerns.

     - o .

AI's transformative power extends beyond borders, revolutionising HR practices worldwide and offering unprecedented opportunities for efficiency, diversity, and personalisation. However, as we embrace these advancements, it's equally important to remain vigilant about the potential risks.

In the next chapter, we will delve into the real-world risks of AI in HR and explore strategies to ensure its safe and ethical use. Join us as we navigate the shadows and uncover ways to mitigate the challenges of AI implementation in HR.

Navigating Risks and Policies in AI

9. Recognising the Shadows: Real-World Risks of AI in HR

Navigating the Risks: Ensuring Safe and Ethical AI in HR

While artificial intelligence (AI) offers numerous benefits for HR processes, it's crucial to understand and address the potential risks associated with its implementation. This chapter will explore these risks and discuss strategies to mitigate them.

Data Privacy and Security

AI systems in HR often handle sensitive employee information, raising significant privacy and security risks. Here are key considerations:

1. **Potential for Data Breaches:**

    - o **Risk:** Unauthorized access to personal data can lead to data breaches.

    - o **Mitigation:** Implement robust cybersecurity measures and comply with data protection regulations like GDPR or CCPA.

2. **Compliance with Regulations:**

    - o **Risk:** Failure to comply with data protection laws can result in legal penalties.

    - o **Mitigation:** Stay informed about evolving data privacy laws and ensure AI systems are compliant.

Algorithmic Bias

AI systems can inadvertently perpetuate or even amplify existing biases in hiring, promotion, and performance evaluation processes:

1. **Bias in Training Data:**

   o **Risk:** Historical biases in training data can lead to unfair or discriminatory decisions.

   o **Mitigation:** Conduct regular audits and use diverse, representative data sets to train AI models.

2. **Bias Detection Mechanisms:**

   o **Risk:** Biased AI algorithms can continue to produce unfair outcomes without regular checks.

   o **Mitigation:** Implement bias detection mechanisms and continuously monitor AI systems for biased behaviour.

Lack of Transparency

Some AI algorithms operate as "black boxes," making it difficult to understand how decisions are made:

1. **Opaque Decision-Making:**

   o **Risk:** Lack of transparency can undermine trust in HR processes.

   o **Mitigation:** Prioritize explainable AI models that provide clear, understandable reasons for decisions.

2. **Human Oversight:**

   o **Risk:** Without human oversight, AI decisions might go unquestioned.

- o **Mitigation:** Maintain human oversight to review AI-generated decisions, especially in complex situations.

Over-Reliance on AI

There's a risk of over-dependence on AI systems, potentially leading to a loss of human judgment and intuition in HR processes:

1. **Loss of Human Judgment:**

   - o **Risk:** Relying too heavily on AI can erode human decision-making skills.

   - o **Mitigation:** Use AI to assist, not replace, human decision-making. Encourage HR professionals to use their judgment and intuition alongside AI insights.

2. **Balancing AI and Human Input:**

   - o **Risk:** Over-reliance on AI might result in neglecting the human aspect of HR.

   - o **Mitigation:** Ensure a balanced approach where AI supports but does not dominate HR processes.

Legal and Regulatory Compliance

The rapid advancement of AI technology often outpaces regulatory frameworks:

1. **Evolving Regulations:**

   - o **Risk:** Keeping up with changing laws can be challenging.

   - o **Mitigation:** Stay informed about legal developments and ensure compliance with relevant regulations.

2. **Legal Risks:**

   o **Risk:** Non-compliance with AI-related laws can lead to legal issues.

   o **Mitigation:** Regularly review and update AI systems to adhere to current laws and regulations.

Employee Trust and Acceptance

Implementing AI in HR processes may lead to employee concerns about job security or privacy:

1. **Job Security Concerns:**

   o **Risk:** Employees may fear job loss due to AI automation.

   o **Mitigation:** Communicate clearly about the role of AI and how it will support rather than replace human jobs.

2. **Privacy Concerns:**

   o **Risk:** Employees may need help with how their data is used.

   o **Mitigation:** Be transparent about data usage and ensure strong privacy protections are in place.

Data Quality and Accuracy

AI systems are only as good as the data they're trained on:

1. **Poor Quality Data:**

   o **Risk:** Inaccurate or poor-quality data can lead to flawed decisions.

- o **Mitigation:** Conduct regular data audits and ensure high-quality data is used for training AI models.

2. **Data Integrity:**

   - o **Risk:** Inaccurate data can undermine AI effectiveness.

   - o **Mitigation:** Implement quality control measures to maintain data integrity.

Ethical Considerations

The use of AI in HR raises ethical questions, particularly around employee monitoring and performance evaluation:

1. **Ethical Guidelines:**

   - o **Risk:** With clear guidelines, the ethical use of AI can be protected.

   - o **Mitigation:** Establish ethical guidelines for AI use and ensure they align with company values and employee rights.

2. **Monitoring and Evaluation:**

   - o **Risk:** Unethical monitoring practices can erode trust.

   - o **Mitigation:** Use AI ethically and transparently, with regular reviews to ensure compliance with ethical standards.

When Not to Use AI

Inappropriate use cases and common mistakes can undermine the effectiveness of AI:

1. **Inappropriate Use Cases:**

   o **Risk:** Using AI that doesn't add value or is unsuitable.

   o **Mitigation:** Evaluate the suitability of AI for each application and avoid using it to appear modern.

2. **Poor ROI:**

   o **Risk:** Implementing AI in scenarios with low return on investment.

   o **Mitigation:** Focus on projects with clear benefits and significant impact.

By recognising these risks, HR leaders can take proactive steps to mitigate them, ensuring that AI implementation enhances rather than compromises HR practices. Responsible AI adoption involves ongoing monitoring, regular audits, and a commitment to maintaining the human touch in HR processes.

In the next chapter, we will explore risk mitigation strategies and how to ensure the ethical use of AI in HR. Join us as we navigate the challenges and solutions in crafting responsible AI policies.

.

10. Safe AI: Strategies for Mitigating Risks and Reducing arm

Mitigating Risks: Strategies for Safe and

As artificial intelligence (AI) systems become more prevalent and powerful, implementing effective strategies for mitigating risks and reducing potential harm is crucial. This chapter will explore various approaches to ensure safer AI development and deployment in HR.

Risk Mitigation and Harm Reduction Strategies

Clear Criteria for Evaluating AI Ideas

Establishing clear criteria before evaluating any AI ideas is essential to ensure alignment with organisational goals and budget constraints:

1. **Establish Criteria:**
   - **Action:** Define specific goals, budget limits, and other relevant factors.
   - **Impact:** This ensures that AI initiatives are feasible and beneficial.
2. **Selection Committee:**
   - **Action:** Form a committee to adhere to these criteria during brainstorming sessions.
   - **Impact:** A committee ensures a structured and objective evaluation process.

Diverse Input

Gathering input from various organisational levels helps gain broader perspectives and generate better ideas:

1. **Inclusive Brainstorming:**
   - **Action:** Include employees from different departments and levels.
   - **Impact:** This approach encourages diverse ideas and prevents a narrow focus on AI use cases.

Human Aspects

Considering morale and other human factors is crucial when deciding on AI use cases:

1. **Recognition and Rewards:**
   - **Action:** Recognize and reward employees who contribute valuable ideas.
   - **Impact:** This boosts morale and encourages active participation.
2. **Employee Engagement:**
   - **Action:** Follow up with people who submit ideas to confirm receipt and provide feedback.
   - **Impact:** Engaging employees fosters a positive culture around AI initiatives.

Expert Advice

Seeking expertise from consultants or specialists can provide valuable insights and guidance:

1. **Consultant Engagement:**
   - **Action:** Hire external experts to advise on AI implementation.
   - **Impact:** Their expertise helps them make informed decisions and avoid common pitfalls.

Avoiding Common Mistakes

Follow-Up and Recognition

Following up with people who submit ideas enhances morale and engagement:

1. **Acknowledgement:**
   - **Action:** Confirm receipt of ideas and recognise contributors.
   - **Impact:** This ensures contributors feel valued and motivated.

Achievable Outcomes

Ensuring that ideas lead to attainable products or proofs of concept within a reasonable timeframe is crucial:

1. **Feasibility Checks:**
   - **Action:** Evaluate ideas for their feasibility and potential to deliver results.
   - **Impact:** This approach focuses efforts on achievable and valuable projects.

Layered Safety Systems

Implementing multiple layers of safety measures provides comprehensive protection:

1. **Model Layer:**
   - **Action:** Choose base models carefully, considering their safety features and limitations.
   - **Impact:** This ensures the foundation of the AI system is secure and reliable.
2. **Safety Systems Layer:**
   - **Action:** Deploy independent AI-based safety systems to monitor inputs and outputs.
   - **Impact:** These systems detect and prevent harmful content and attacks.
3. **User Experience Layer:**
   - **Action:** Design user interfaces that guide users towards intended use and prevent misuse.
   - **Impact:** This helps maintain safe and effective AI interactions.

Robust Testing and Evaluation

Conducting thorough testing of AI systems before deployment is crucial:

1. **Diverse Datasets:**
   - o **Action:** Use diverse datasets to evaluate model performance.
   - o **Impact:** This ensures the AI system performs well across different scenarios.
2. **Regular Audits:**
   - o **Action:** Implement regular audits to detect bias, errors, or unexpected behaviours.
   - o **Impact:** This helps maintain the integrity and fairness of AI systems.

Transparency and Explainability

Prioritising transparency in AI decision-making builds trust:

1. **Explainable AI:**
   - o **Action:** Use explainable AI models, especially for high-stakes applications.
   - o **Impact:** This explains AI decisions clearly to users and stakeholders.
2. **Detailed Documentation:**
   - o **Action:** Maintain detailed documentation of model architecture, training data, and decision processes.
   - o **Impact:** This ensures accountability and transparency.

Continuous Monitoring and Improvement

Ongoing monitoring and improvement are essential for safe AI systems:

1. **Real-Time Monitoring:**
   - o **Action:** Set up real-time monitoring to detect performance issues.
   - o **Impact:** This ensures timely identification and resolution of problems.
2. **Feedback Loops:**
   - o **Action:** Establish feedback loops to incorporate user experiences and outcomes.
   - o **Impact:** This helps continuously improve AI systems.

Ethical Guidelines and Governance

Strong ethical guidelines and governance structures are critical:

1. **Ethical Principles:**
   - **Action:** Establish clear ethical principles for AI development and use.
   - **Impact:** This ensures AI aligns with organisational values and employee rights.
2. **AI Ethics Board:**
   - **Action:** Create an AI ethics board to oversee projects and address ethical concerns.
   - **Impact:** This provides oversight and ensures responsible AI use.

Conducting comprehensive risk assessments helps identify and mitigate potential risks:

1. **Risk Identification:**
   - **Action:** Identify risks across various categories, including individual, societal, and environmental impacts.
   - **Impact:** This ensures all potential risks are considered.
2. **Specific Controls:**
   - **Action:** Develop specific controls and strategies for each identified risk.
   - **Impact:** This provides targeted risk mitigation.

Human Oversight and Control

Maintaining meaningful human involvement is crucial for safe AI deployment:

1. **Human-in-the-Loop Systems:**
   - **Action:** Implement systems where humans can oversee and override AI decisions.
   - **Impact:** This ensures critical decisions involve human judgment.
2. **Employee Training:**
   - **Action:** Train employees to work alongside AI systems effectively.

- o **Impact:** This ensures they can safely and efficiently use AI.

Data Security and Privacy

Protecting sensitive data is essential for maintaining trust and compliance:

1. **Cybersecurity Measures:**
   - o **Action:** Implement robust cybersecurity measures to prevent data breaches.
   - o **Impact:** This protects sensitive employee information.
2. **Data Protection Regulations:**
   - o **Action:** Ensure compliance with data protection laws like GDPR.
   - o **Impact:** This ensures legal compliance and protects employee privacy.

Collaboration and Knowledge Sharing

Fostering collaboration within the AI community enhances safety and ethics:

1. **Industry Initiatives:**
   - o **Action:** Participate in industry-wide initiatives focused on AI safety.
   - o **Impact:** This promotes best practices and knowledge sharing.
2. **Policymaker Engagement:**
   - o **Action:** Engage with policymakers to shape responsible AI governance.
   - o **Impact:** This ensures practical insights inform regulatory frameworks.

Education and Awareness

Promoting understanding of AI risks and benefits is crucial for responsible use:

1. **Employee Education:**
   - o **Action:** Educate employees about AI capabilities and limitations.
   - o **Impact:** This ensures they can use AI responsibly.
2. **Clear Communication:**
   - o **Action:** Communicate clearly about the role of AI in your organisation.
   - o **Impact:** This builds trust and understanding.

By implementing these strategies, organisations can significantly mitigate risks associated with AI systems and work towards reducing potential harm. It's important to remember that AI safety is an ongoing process that requires constant vigilance, adaptation, and improvement as technology evolves and new challenges emerge.

The next chapter will explore creating and enforcing AI regulations and policies. Join us as we navigate the complexities of crafting responsible AI governance.

11. Setting the Rules: Regulatory Frameworks for AI in HR

Navigating the Regulatory Landscape: Ensuring Fair and Ethical AI in HR

As artificial intelligence (AI) becomes increasingly integral to HR processes, it is essential to have robust frameworks to ensure its ethical and fair use. This chapter delves into key AI implementation frameworks and their implications for businesses.

Key AI Implementation Frameworks

NIST AI Risk Management Framework (AI RMF)

- **Developed by**: U.S. National Institute of Standards and Technology
- **Focus**: Identifying and managing risks associated with AI systems
- **Purpose**: Provides a comprehensive approach to trustworthy and responsible AI

European Union's AI Act

- **Proposed by**: European Union
- **Focus**: Regulating AI systems within the EU
- **Purpose**: Ensures AI systems are safe, transparent, traceable, non-discriminatory, and environmentally friendly
- **Categories**: AI systems are categorised based on risk levels with corresponding rules

OECD AI Principles

- **Adopted by** OECD member countries in 2019
- **Focus**: Promoting innovative, trustworthy AI that respects human rights and democratic values
- **Purpose**: Provides recommendations for public policy and AI governance

IEEE Ethically Aligned Design

- **Focus**: Prioritizing human wellbeing with autonomous and intelligent systems
- **Topics**: Addresses data agency, transparency, and accountability in AI systems

Singapore's Model AI Governance Framework

- **Focus**: Detailed guidance for private sector organizations
- **Purpose**: Provides practical advice on internal governance structures, decision-making models, and operations management

Key Components of AI Implementation Frameworks

These frameworks typically cover several crucial aspects:

1. **Governance**: Establishing oversight and accountability structures
2. **Risk Assessment**: Identifying and mitigating potential harms
3. **Transparency**: Ensuring AI systems are explainable and their decision-making processes are clear
4. **Fairness and Non-discrimination**: Preventing and addressing bias in AI systems
5. **Privacy and Data Governance**: Protecting personal data and ensuring responsible data use
6. **Safety and Security**: Ensuring AI systems are robust and secure
7. **Human Oversight**: Maintaining appropriate human control over AI systems
8. **Accountability**: Establishing clear lines of responsibility for AI outcomes

Challenges in AI Implementation Frameworks

Implementing these frameworks comes with its own set of challenges:

1. **Keeping Pace with Rapid Technological Advancements**: Ensuring frameworks remain relevant as technology evolves
2. **Balancing Innovation with Regulation**: Encouraging innovation while maintaining regulatory standards
3. **Addressing Cross-Border and Cross-Sector Challenges**: Managing AI's impact across different regions and industries

4. **Ensuring Flexibility**: Creating frameworks that are adaptable to diverse AI applications
5. **Harmonising Different Approaches**: Aligning various national and regional regulatory frameworks

AI implementation frameworks are crucial for ensuring that AI systems in HR are ethical, fair, and beneficial. By following these frameworks, organisations can navigate the complex landscape of AI regulation and ensure their AI systems align with societal values.

The next chapter will explore specific regulations currently in place and those emerging globally. Join us as we delve into these regulatory frameworks' detailed requirements and implications.

.

12. Current and Emerging Regulations

Current and Emerging Regulations

European Union AI Act

The European Parliament recently approved the EU AI Act, classifying AI use in employment as high-risk. This legislation has significant implications:

1. **Avoid High-Risk Solutions:**
   - **Requirement:** HR professionals must avoid AI solutions that use biometric data or provide subjective information on emotion or sentiment.
   - **Impact:** Ensures AI systems do not infringe on employee privacy or make biased decisions.
2. **Maintain Human Oversight:**
   - **Requirement:** Avoid solutions that remove human oversight from hiring decisions.
   - **Impact:** Ensures fairness and accountability in HR processes.
3. **Transparency and Documentation:**
   - **Requirement:** Employers must ensure transparency, maintain documentation, and implement bias reduction measures.
   - **Impact:** Promotes trust and ethical use of AI in HR.

Canada's Artificial Intelligence and Data Act (AIDA)

Set to be enforced in 2025, AIDA will regulate high-impact AI systems in Canada. For HR, this means:

1. **Privacy and Fairness:**
   - **Requirement:** AI tools used in employment must meet privacy, transparency, and fairness requirements.
   - **Impact:** Protects employee rights and promotes ethical AI use.

United States Regulations

While there's no comprehensive federal AI law in the U.S. yet, several state-level developments are noteworthy:

1. **State-Level Legislation:**
   - **Trend:** An increasing number of state laws focus on AI regulation in HR.
   - **Impact:** Businesses must stay informed and compliant with varying state regulations.
2. **New York City's AI Law:**
   - **Legislation:** The first workplace AI law in the nation, potentially setting a precedent for other jurisdictions.
   - **Impact:** This may influence AI regulations across the country.
3. **EEOC Guidance:**
   - **Guidance:** The U.S. Equal Employment Opportunity Commission has issued guidance on how anti-discrimination laws apply to AI in employment decisions.
   - **Impact:** Ensures AI systems do not violate anti-discrimination laws.

Implications for Businesses

Compliance Complexity

With the proliferation of state-level regulations in the U.S. and varying international standards, businesses face a complex compliance landscape:

1. **Multi-Jurisdictional Compliance:**
   - **Challenge:** Ensuring compliance with diverse regulations across different regions.
   - **Strategy:** Regularly review and update AI systems to meet legal requirements.

Increased Scrutiny

Employers will be held responsible for any discriminatory impact of AI:

1. **Accountability:**
   - **Requirement:** HR departments must regularly audit AI systems for bias and discriminatory outcomes.
   - **Impact:** Ensures fair and equitable AI-driven HR processes.

Vendor Management

HR departments need to review all vendor relationships:

1. **Vendor Compliance:**
   - **Action:** Ensure AI vendors comply with relevant regulations.
   - **Impact:** Protects the organisation from legal risks associated with third-party AI tools.

Transparency Requirements

Many regulations emphasise the need for transparency in AI decision-making processes:

1. **Clear Explanations:**
   - **Requirement:** Ensure AI systems can provide clear explanations for decisions.
   - **Impact:** Builds trust and accountability in AI-driven HR processes.

Data Privacy Focus

Regulations like GDPR continue to play a crucial role:

1. **Data Protection:**
   - **Requirement:** Ensure all AI-driven data processing complies with data protection laws.
   - **Impact:** Safeguards employee privacy and meets legal standards.

Bias Audits

Regular audits and impact assessments of AI systems may become mandatory:

1. **Bias Detection:**
   - **Action:** Conduct regular bias audits to detect and mitigate potential biases.
   - **Impact:** Ensures fair and unbiased AI outcomes.

Human Oversight

Most regulations stress the importance of human review in AI-generated decisions:

1. **Human Review:**
   - **Requirement:** Maintain human oversight in critical decision-making areas.
   - **Impact:** Ensures ethical and responsible AI use.

As AI continues to evolve, regulatory frameworks will likely undergo frequent updates. HR leaders must remain agile, continuously reassessing their AI strategies to ensure compliance while leveraging these benefits. Businesses can build trust with employees and candidates while optimising their HR processes by prioritising ethical AI use and staying ahead of regulatory requirements.

The next chapter will explore building trust by developing ethical AI policies for HR. Join us as we explore the critical steps in establishing ethical standards and ensuring transparency in AI-driven HR processes.

13. Building Trust: Developing Ethical AI Policies for HR

Ensuring Responsible AI Use: Crafting Ethical Policies for HR

Creating and implementing responsible AI policies is crucial for organisations to ensure the ethical use of artificial intelligence in HR processes. This chapter outlines the necessity of developing AI policies that are not only effective but also ethical and responsible. It emphasises the role of these policies in building trust within the organisation and with external stakeholders.

The Necessity of Ethical AI Policies

Developing responsible AI policies is essential for:

1. **Building Trust:**
   - **Goal:** Establish trust within the organisation and with external stakeholders.
   - **Impact:** Transparent and ethical AI policies help gain the confidence of employees and stakeholders.
2. **Ensuring Fairness:**
   - **Goal:** Ensure that AI technologies are used in a manner that is fair, transparent, and accountable.
   - **Impact:** Mitigates risks of bias and discrimination.
3. **Promoting Ethical Use:**
   - **Goal:** Address broader ethical implications of AI use.
   - **Impact:** Ensures AI applications do not negatively affect employees, customers, or society.

Implementation Strategies

Forming an AI Task Force

1. **Create a Cross-Functional Team:**
   - **Action:** Include representatives from HR, IT, Legal, and other relevant departments.

- o **Impact:** Ensures the policy addresses needs across the organisation.

Defining Scope and Purpose

1. **Outline Objectives:**
   - o **Action:** Specify which AI technologies and applications are covered.
   - o **Impact:** Provides clear guidance on responsible AI use within HR.
2. **Explain Purpose:**
   - o **Action:** Define the policy's purpose in guiding ethical AI use.
   - o **Impact:** Aligns AI initiatives with organisational values.

Best Practices for Responsible AI Policies

Establishing Ethical Guidelines

1. **Develop Ethical Principles:**
   - o **Action:** Prohibit the creation of misleading, fraudulent, or harmful content.
   - o **Impact:** Ensures AI use aligns with ethical standards.
2. **Ensure Transparency:**
   - o **Action:** AI-generated content is required to be marked as such.
   - o **Impact:** Promotes honesty and clarity.
3. **Address Bias and Discrimination:**
   - o **Action:** Implement steps for identifying and mitigating bias.
   - o **Impact:** Ensures fair and equitable outcomes.

Data Management and Privacy

1. **Implement Data Handling Procedures:**
   - o **Action:** Obtain explicit consent before using personal data for AI tasks.

- o **Impact:** Protects employee privacy.
2. **Adhere to Data Protection Laws:**
   - o **Action:** Comply with relevant data protection regulations.
   - o **Impact:** Ensures legal compliance.

Defining Permissible Use

1. **Specify AI Use in HR:**
   - o **Action:** Outline which employees or departments are authorised to use AI tools.
   - o **Impact:** Ensures controlled and appropriate use of AI.
2. **Determine Specific Tasks:**
   - o **Action:** Define tasks that may be performed using AI.
   - o **Impact:** Prevents misuse and ensures focused application.

Accountability Measures

Ensuring Responsibility for AI Outcomes

1. **Assign Accountability:**
   - o **Action:** Make employees accountable for AI-generated outcomes.
   - o **Impact:** Ensures human oversight and responsibility.
2. **Require Fact-Checking:**
   - o **Action:** Mandate fact-checking and bias verification of AI-generated content.
   - o **Impact:** Maintains accuracy and fairness.

Protecting Confidential Information

Safeguarding Sensitive Data

1. **Prohibit Submissions of Confidential Data:**
   - o **Action:** Ban submitting trade secrets and other confidential information to AI tools.
   - o **Impact:** Protects company secrets.
2. **Define Confidential Information:**

- o **Action:** Clearly define what constitutes confidential information.
- o **Impact:** Prevents accidental disclosure.

Implementing Oversight and Governance

Monitoring AI Use

1. **Designate Oversight Roles:**
   - o **Action:** Assign an individual or department to oversee AI use.
   - o **Impact:** Ensures proper governance.
2. **Establish Reporting Mechanisms:**
   - o **Action:** Implement the use of logs or reporting mechanisms.
   - o **Impact:** Enhances transparency.

Legal Compliance

Adhering to Laws and Regulations

1. **Conduct Legal Reviews:**
   - o **Action:** Ensure AI use complies with copyright, privacy, and intellectual property laws.
   - o **Impact:** Prevents legal infringements.
2. **Stay Informed:**
   - o **Action:** Keep up-to-date with evolving AI regulations.
   - o **Impact:** Ensures ongoing compliance.

Training and Awareness

Educating Employees on AI Use

1. **Provide Regular Training:**
   - o **Action:** Educate employees on the AI policy and ethical considerations.
   - o **Impact:** Promotes responsible AI use.
2. **Encourage Communication:**

- o **Action:** Managers should frequently communicate AI expectations.
- o **Impact:** Ensures understanding and compliance.

Review and Update

Keeping Policies Current

1. **Annual Reviews:**
   - o **Action:** Review and update the AI policy annually or as needed.
   - o **Impact:** Keeps policies relevant and effective.
2. **Adapt to Changes:**
   - o **Action:** Remain agile to adapt to technological and legal changes.
   - o **Impact:** Ensures continuous improvement.

Enforcement and Reporting

Establishing Consequences for Violations

1. **Outline Disciplinary Actions:**
   - o **Action:** Define consequences for non-compliance.
   - o **Impact:** Ensures adherence to the policy.
2. **Create Reporting Mechanisms:**
   - o **Action:** Implement mechanisms for reporting violations.
   - o **Impact:** Encourages accountability.

By implementing these guidelines, organizations can create a robust framework for ethical AI use in HR. This approach mitigates risks and builds trust with employees and stakeholders. Remember, crafting an AI policy is an ongoing process that requires continuous evaluation and refinement as AI technologies and their applications evolve.

The next chapter will explore how to prepare your HR team for the AI revolution. Join us as we delve into comprehensive steps for effective AI integration, ensuring your HR team is ready for tomorrow's challenges and opportunities.

.

Implementing AI in HR: Practical Steps

14. Ready for Tomorrow: Preparing Your HR Team for AI

Equipping HR for the AI Revolution: Steps for Effective Integration

As AI reshapes the HR landscape, HR teams must proactively prepare for this technological shift. Here's a comprehensive guide to help your HR team prepare for AI integration.

Steps for Preparing HR Teams for AI Integration

1. Assess Current Skills and Identify Gaps

Start by evaluating your team's existing skills and knowledge related to AI:

1. **Conduct a Skills Audit:**
   - **Action:** Determine your HR team's current level of AI literacy.
   - **Impact:** Identifies key areas where upskilling is needed, such as data analysis, AI ethics, and basic programming concepts.

2. Develop a Comprehensive Training Program

Create a tailored learning program to bridge the identified skill gaps:

1. **Offer AI Fundamentals Courses:**
   - **Action:** Provide AI fundamentals, machine learning, and data analytics courses.
   - **Impact:** Equips the team with necessary AI knowledge.
2. **Training on Specific AI Tools:**
   - **Action:** Offer training on AI tools and platforms relevant to HR functions.
   - **Impact:** Ensures the team can effectively use AI technologies in their roles.
3. **Include AI Ethics Modules:**

- o **Action:** Incorporate modules on AI ethics and responsible AI use.
- o **Impact:** Promotes ethical considerations in AI applications.

3. Foster a Data-Driven Culture

Encourage a mindset shift towards data-driven decision-making:

1. **Promote Data Literacy:**
   - o **Action:** Emphasize the importance of data literacy across the HR team.
   - o **Impact:** Facilitates better decision-making based on data insights.
2. **Implement Data Visualization Tools:**
   - o **Action:** Use tools to make data insights more accessible.
   - o **Impact:** Enhances understanding and usage of data.

4. Collaborate with IT and Data Science Teams

Build strong partnerships with technical teams:

1. **Knowledge-Sharing Sessions:**
   - o **Action:** Establish regular sessions between HR and IT/data science teams.
   - o **Impact:** Encourages cross-functional learning and collaboration.
2. **Create Cross-Functional Project Teams:**
   - o **Action:** Form teams for AI initiatives.
   - o **Impact:** Ensures diverse expertise in AI projects.

5. Pilot AI Projects

Start small and scale up:

1. **Identify Low-Risk Areas:**
   - o **Action:** Implement AI in low-risk areas as pilot projects.
   - o **Impact:** Provides hands-on experience and helps refine strategies.
2. **Involve HR Team Members:**
   - o **Action:** Engage HR professionals in these pilots.

- o **Impact:** Builds practical AI skills within the team.

6. Develop AI Governance Frameworks

Establish clear guidelines for AI use within HR:

1. **Create Ethical AI Policies:**
   - o **Action:** Develop policies for ethical AI use, data privacy, and transparency.
   - o **Impact:** Ensures responsible AI implementation.
2. **Define Roles and Responsibilities:**
   - o **Action:** Assign roles for AI oversight within the HR team.
   - o **Impact:** Provides clear accountability.

7. Focus on Change Management

Prepare your team and the broader organisation for the changes AI will bring:

1. **Communicate Clearly:**
   - o **Action:** Explain the role and benefits of AI in HR.
   - o **Impact:** Reduces fears and misconceptions about AI.
2. **Address Concerns:**
   - o **Action:** Highlight how AI will augment human capabilities rather than replace them.
   - o **Impact:** Builds confidence in AI integration.

8. Redefine HR Roles and Responsibilities

Adapt job descriptions and team structures to incorporate AI:

1. **Create New AI-Focused Roles:**
   - o **Action:** Develop roles focused on AI strategy and implementation.
   - o **Impact:** Ensures specialised attention to AI initiatives.
2. **Modify Existing Roles:**
   - o **Action:** Include AI-related responsibilities in current job descriptions.
   - o **Impact:** Integrates AI tasks into daily HR functions.

9. Encourage Continuous Learning

Foster a culture of ongoing education and adaptation:

1. **Provide Learning Resources:**
   - **

- **Action:** Offer resources for self-paced learning about AI advancements.
   - **Impact:** Keeps the team updated with the latest AI developments.

1. **Attend AI Conferences and Workshops:**
   - **Action:** Encourage team members to attend relevant events.
   - **Impact:** Enhances knowledge and networking opportunities.
2. **Internal Knowledge-Sharing Platform:**
   - **Action:** Set up a platform for sharing AI-related insights and best practices.
   - **Impact:** Promotes continuous learning and collaboration within the team.

10. Develop AI-Human Collaboration Skills

Prepare your team to work alongside AI systems:

1. **Train on AI Interpretation:**
   - **Action:** Train HR professionals to interpret and act on AI-generated insights.
   - **Impact:** Ensures effective use of AI data in decision-making.
2. **Overseeing AI Decisions:**
   - **Action:** Develop skills for overseeing and validating AI-driven decisions.
   - **Impact:** Maintains human judgment in critical processes.
3. **Emphasise Human Judgment:**
   - **Action:** Highlight the importance of combining AI capabilities with human judgment.
   - **Impact:** Ensures a balanced approach to AI integration.

11. Stay Informed About AI Regulations

Keep your team updated on the evolving regulatory landscape:

1. **Monitor AI Legislation:**
   - **Action:** Assign team members to keep track of AI-related laws and guidelines.
   - **Impact:** Ensures compliance with new regulations.
2. **Regular Policy Updates:**
   - **Action:** Regularly update AI policies to reflect legal changes.
   - **Impact:** Keeps the organisation aligned with regulatory requirements.
3. **Industry Forums:**
   - **Action:** Participate in discussions about AI governance in HR.
   - **Impact:** Provides insights into best practices and emerging trends.

12. Measure and Communicate Impact

Track the effectiveness of your AI integration efforts:

1. **Establish KPIs:**
   - **Action:** Set key performance indicators for AI initiatives.
   - **Impact:** Measures the success and impact of AI projects.
2. **Regular Reporting:**
   - **Action:** Report on AI's impact on HR efficiency and effectiveness.
   - **Impact:** Demonstrates the value of AI to stakeholders.
3. **Share Success Stories:**
   - **Action:** Use success stories to build enthusiasm and support for AI adoption.
   - **Impact:** Encourages broader acceptance and engagement with AI.

By following these steps, HR teams can position themselves at the forefront of AI integration, ensuring they are well-prepared to leverage AI technologies effectively and responsibly. The goal is not just to implement AI but to create a symbiotic relationship between human expertise and AI capabilities, ultimately enhancing the strategic value of HR within the organisation.

The next chapter will guide you through starting small with your first AI use case. Join us as we provide a comprehensive roadmap to help you identify, plan, and execute your initial AI project in HR, setting the stage for broader AI adoption.

15. Starting Small: Your First AI Use Case

Starting Small: Identifying and Implementing Your First AI Use Case

Implementing your first AI project in HR is a critical step towards broader AI adoption. Here's a comprehensive roadmap to help you identify, plan, and execute your initial AI use case.

Identifying the First AI Use Case

1. Assess Needs and Opportunities

Start by exploring areas where AI can add immediate value within HR:

1. **Analyse Current HR Processes:**
   - **Action:** Identify bottlenecks or inefficiencies in existing HR workflows.
   - **Impact:** Highlights areas where AI can make a significant difference.
2. **Consult with HR Team Members:**
   - **Action:** Gather ideas and feedback on pain points that AI could address.
   - **Impact:** Ensures the selected use case aligns with real needs.
3. **Consider Common AI Applications:**
   - **Examples:**
     - Resume screening and candidate matching
     - Chatbots for employee queries
     - Predictive analytics for employee turnover
     - Automated scheduling for interviews

2. Define Objectives

Clearly define the objectives for the AI project:

1. **Set Specific Goals:**
   - **Action:** Define SMART (Specific, Measurable, Achievable, Relevant, Time-bound) goals.

- o **Impact:** Provides clear direction and measurable outcomes.
2. **Identify Expected Benefits:**
   - o **Action:** Determine the benefits such as time savings, improved accuracy, or enhanced employee experience.
   - o **Impact:** Aligns the project with organisational priorities.

Planning the AI Project

3. Feasibility Study

Conduct a feasibility study to evaluate the technical and economic viability of the AI project:

1. **Evaluate Data Requirements:**
   - o **Action:** Assess the availability and quality of necessary data.
   - o **Impact:** Ensures the project has a solid data foundation.
2. **Assess Available Resources:**
   - o **Action:** Determine the resources needed, including personnel and technology.
   - o **Impact:** Identifies potential gaps that need addressing.
3. **Estimate Potential Costs:**
   - o **Action:** Calculate the financial investment required.
   - o **Impact:** Ensures the project is economically viable.

4. Develop a Project Plan

Create a detailed project plan outlining the steps needed to implement the AI solution:

1. **Outline Timelines:**
   - o **Action:** Set realistic deadlines for each phase of the project.
   - o **Impact:** Keeps the project on track.
2. **Allocate Resources:**
   - o **Action:** Assign team members and allocate necessary resources.
   - o **Impact:** Ensures all aspects of the project are covered.
3. **Set Key Milestones:**
   - o **Action:** Identify critical points for progress checks.

- o **Impact:** Helps monitor and manage progress.

Executing the AI Project

5. Pilot Testing

Start with a pilot test of the AI solution on a small scale:

1. **Implement a Prototype:**
   - o **Action:** Create a minimal viable product (MVP) of the AI solution.
   - o **Impact:** Allows for initial testing and feedback gathering.
2. **Gather Feedback:**
   - o **Action:** Collect input from a limited user group.
   - o **Impact:** Identifies any issues and areas for improvement.

6. Full Implementation

Once the pilot is successful, proceed with the full implementation of the AI project:

1. **Roll Out the AI Tool:**
   - o **Action:** Deploy the AI solution across the HR department.
   - o **Impact:** Ensures AI enhances all relevant processes.
2. **Train Stakeholders:**
   - o **Action:** Provide training for HR staff on using the new AI tools.
   - o **Impact:** Ensures effective and confident use of AI technology.

7. Monitoring and Evaluation

Continuously monitor the AI system's performance and evaluate its impact on HR processes:

1. **Track Performance Metrics:**
   - o **Action:** Measure efficiency improvements, cost savings, and user satisfaction.

- o **Impact:** Gauges the success of the AI implementation.
2. **Conduct Regular Reviews:**
   - o **Action:** Schedule periodic evaluations to assess the system's performance.
   - o **Impact:** Ensures the AI solution remains effective and aligned with goals.

8. Stakeholder Engagement

Engage stakeholders from the beginning to ensure buy-in and support for the AI project:

1. **Communicate Progress:**
   - o **Action:** Regularly update stakeholders on project developments.
   - o **Impact:** Keeps everyone informed and aligned.
2. **Address Concerns:**
   - o **Action:** Promptly tackle any issues or worries.
   - o **Impact:** Maintains support and trust in the project.

9. Training and Support

Provide comprehensive training and ongoing support to HR staff:

1. **Develop Training Materials:**
   - o **Action:** Create resources to help staff understand and use AI tools.
   - o **Impact:** Ensures smooth adoption and effective use.
2. **Offer Continuous Support:**
   - o **Action:** Provide ongoing assistance and troubleshooting.
   - o **Impact:** Maintains confidence and competence in AI usage.

10. Continuous Improvement

AI implementation is an iterative process. Continuously seek feedback and make necessary adjustments:

1. **Gather User Feedback:**
   - o **Action:** Regularly collect input from AI tool users.
   - o **Impact:** Identifies areas for improvement.

2. **Refine AI Models:**
   - **Action:** Update and enhance AI systems based on feedback and performance data.
   - **Impact:** Ensures the AI solution remains relevant and practical.

By starting small and focusing on the initial use case, organisations can gain valuable experience and build confidence in AI implementation within their HR processes. The first project aims to solve a specific problem, gain valuable insights, and lay the foundation for broader AI adoption.

The next chapter will explore strategies for successfully deploying AI in HR and managing organisational change. Join us as we delve into the practical steps for seamless AI integration and maximising the benefits of AI technologies.

.

16. Smooth Transitions: Deploying AI and Managing Change

Building Trust and Navigating Organizational Change for Seamless AI Integration in HR

Successfully deploying AI in HR requires a strategic approach that builds stakeholder trust and effectively manages organisational change. Here are key strategies to ensure a smooth transition.

Strategies for Successfully Deploying AI in HR

1. Develop a Clear AI Strategy

Start with a well-defined plan:

1. **Align AI Initiatives with Business Objectives:**
   - **Action:** Ensure AI projects support the overall goals of the organisation.
   - **Impact:** Creates a coherent strategy that benefits the entire company.
2. **Identify Beneficial HR Processes:**
   - **Action:** Pinpoint specific HR functions where AI can add value.
   - **Impact:** Focuses efforts on areas with the highest potential impact.
3. **Set Realistic Goals and Timelines:**
   - **Action:** Establish achievable milestones and deadlines.
   - **Impact:** Keeps the project on track and manageable.

2. Communicate Transparently

Open and honest communication is crucial:

1. **Explain Reasons for AI Adoption:**
   - **Action:** Clearly articulate the benefits and goals of AI implementation.
   - **Impact:** Builds understanding and support among employees.
2. **Address Job Security Concerns:**

- o **Action:** Reassure employees about their job security and how AI will support rather than replace them.
- o **Impact:** Reduces fear and resistance to change.
3. **Regular Updates:**
   - o **Action:** Keep employees informed about the progress of AI initiatives.
   - o **Impact:** Maintains engagement and transparency.

3. Involve Stakeholders Early

Engage critical players from the beginning:

1. **Include Cross-Functional Teams:**
   - o **Action:** Involve HR, IT, legal, and other relevant departments in planning.
   - o **Impact:** Ensures diverse perspectives and expertise.
2. **Seek Employee Input:**
   - o **Action:** Gather feedback from those who will use the AI tools.
   - o **Impact:** Enhances relevance and acceptance of AI solutions.
3. **Form an AI Steering Committee:**
   - o **Action:** Create a committee to oversee AI implementation.
   - o **Impact:** Provides guidance and oversight.

4. Provide Comprehensive Training

Equip employees with the necessary skills:

1. **Offer Training Programs:**
   - o **Action:** Provide sessions on how to use and interact with AI tools.
   - o **Impact:** Ensures competence and confidence in using new technologies.
2. **Resources for Continuous Learning:**
   - o **Action:** Offer ongoing education and resources as AI evolves.
   - o **Impact:** Keeps skills up-to-date.
3. **Create AI Champions:**

- o **Action:** Designate knowledgeable employees to support others.
- o **Impact:** Facilitates peer learning and support.

5. Start with Pilot Projects

Begin with small-scale implementations:

1. **Choose a Specific HR Function:**
   - o **Action:** Select a manageable area for initial AI deployment.
   - o **Impact:** Provides a focused environment for testing and learning.
2. **Gather Feedback and Iterate:**
   - o **Action:** Use pilot projects to gather data and improve the solution.
   - o **Impact:** Refines the AI application before a broader rollout.

6. Ensure Ethical AI Use

Build trust through responsible AI practices:

1. **Develop Ethical Guidelines:**
   - o **Action:** Create policies for ethical AI use in HR.
   - o **Impact:** Ensures fairness and accountability.
2. **Prevent Bias:**
   - o **Action:** Implement measures to detect and prevent bias in AI decisions.
   - o **Impact:** Promotes equity and trust in AI systems.
3. **Regular Audits:**
   - o **Action:** Conduct audits to ensure AI systems are fair and transparent.
   - o **Impact:** Maintains integrity and trust.

Building Trust with Stakeholders

7. Maintain Human Oversight

Balance AI capabilities with human judgment:

1. **Define Human Roles:**
   - **Action:** Specify areas where human decision-making is essential.
   - **Impact:** Ensures humans oversee critical decisions.
2. **Implement Human-in-the-Loop Processes:**
   - **Action:** Incorporate human oversight in AI-driven processes.
   - **Impact:** Enhances reliability and trust.

8. Address Data Privacy Concerns

Prioritise data protection:

1. **Transparent Data Use:**
   - **Action:** Communicate data collection and usage policies.
   - **Impact:** Builds trust through transparency.
2. **Compliance with Regulations:**
   - **Action:** Ensure AI systems comply with data privacy laws.
   - **Impact:** Protects employee data and meets legal requirements.
3. **Robust Security Measures:**
   - **Action:** Implement strong data security protocols.
   - **Impact:** Safeguards sensitive information.

Managing Organizational Change

9. Develop a Change Management Plan

Prepare your team and the organisation for AI integration:

1. **Comprehensive Plan:**
   - **Action:** Address impacts on workflows, job roles, and culture.
   - **Impact:** Ensures a smooth transition.
2. **Strategies for Managing Resistance:**

- o **Action:** Develop approaches to handle resistance to change.
- o **Impact:** Facilitates acceptance and adaptation.

10. Provide Ongoing Support

Offer continuous assistance:

1. **Dedicated Support Team:**
   - o **Action:** Set up a team to address AI-related queries.
   - o **Impact:** Provides help and reassurance.
2. **User-Friendly Documentation:**
   - o **Action:** Create clear and accessible documentation.
   - o **Impact:** Supports understanding and usage.
3. **Feedback Mechanisms:**
   - o **Action:** Establish channels for ongoing feedback.
   - o **Impact:** Enables continuous improvement.

11. Manage Expectations

Set realistic expectations about AI capabilities:

1. **Communicate Capabilities and Limitations:**
   - o **Action:** Clearly explain what AI can and cannot do.
   - o **Impact:** Prevents misunderstandings and over-promising.
2. **Discuss Potential Setbacks:**
   - o **Action:** Be open about possible challenges.
   - o **Impact:** Builds resilience and readiness.

12. Foster a Culture of Innovation

Encourage an adaptive mindset:

1. **Promote Technological Change:**
   - o **Action:** Foster a culture that embraces innovation.
   - o **Impact:** Encourages acceptance of new technologies.
2. **Recognise AI Use:**
   - o **Action:** Reward effective use of AI tools.
   - o **Impact:** Motivates and inspires employees.
3. **Encourage Experimentation:**

- o **Action:** Support trying new approaches and learning from failures.
- o **Impact:** Drives continuous improvement and innovation.

Best Practices for AI Deployment

13. Plan for Scalability

Prepare for future expansion:

1. **Scalable AI Solutions:**
   - o **Action:** Choose AI tools that can grow with the organisation.
   - o **Impact:** Ensures long-term usability.
2. **Integration Roadmap:**
   - o **Action:** Develop a plan for integrating AI across HR functions.
   - o **Impact:** Facilitates smooth expansion.

Successfully deploying AI in HR requires a strategic approach that builds stakeholder trust and effectively manages organisational change. By following these strategies, organisations can ensure a smooth transition and maximise the benefits of AI technologies.

The next chapter will focus on continuous improvement, monitoring, and evaluating AI systems to ensure they remain effective and aligned with organisational goals. Join us as we explore methods for maintaining and enhancing AI-driven HR processes.

17. Continuous Improvement: Monitoring and Evaluating AI in HR

Ensuring Longevity: Continuous Monitoring and Improvement of AI in HR

Effectively monitoring and evaluating AI systems in HR ensures their ongoing effectiveness, fairness, and alignment with organisational goals. Here's a comprehensive approach to measuring performance and driving continuous improvement.

Metrics for Evaluating AI Performance

1. Efficiency Metrics

Measure how much time and resources are saved by using AI:

1. **Time-to-Hire Reduction:**
   - **Action:** Track the average hiring time before and after AI implementation.
   - **Impact:** Measures the efficiency of AI in streamlining the recruitment process.
2. **Cost-per-Hire Decrease:**
   - **Action:** Calculate the cost savings in the hiring process due to AI automation.
   - **Impact:** Assesses the economic benefit of AI in HR.
3. **Automation Rate of HR Tasks:**
   - **Action:** Measure the percentage of HR tasks automated by AI.
   - **Impact:** Indicates the level of process automation achieved.

2. Effectiveness Metrics

Assess the accuracy and quality of AI outputs:

1. **Quality of Hire Improvement:**
   - **Action:** Evaluate hires' performance and retention rates using AI tools.

- o **Impact:** Determines the effectiveness of AI in improving hiring decisions.
2. **Employee Retention Rate:**
   - o **Action:** Compare retention rates before and after AI implementation in HR processes.
   - o **Impact:** Indicates the long-term impact of AI on employee satisfaction and retention.
3. **Diversity and Inclusion Metrics:**
   - o **Action:** Track diversity in hiring and promotions to ensure AI tools promote inclusivity.
   - o **Impact:** Measures the fairness and inclusiveness of AI-driven HR processes.

3. Engagement Metrics

Evaluate how AI tools affect employee engagement and satisfaction:

1. **HR Team Satisfaction with AI Tools:**
   - o **Action:** Conduct surveys to gather feedback from HR staff on their experience with AI tools.
   - o **Impact:** Gauges the acceptance and usability of AI technologies.
2. **Employee Satisfaction with AI-Driven Processes:**
   - o **Action:** Survey employees to assess their satisfaction with AI-enabled HR processes.
   - o **Impact:** Ensures that AI tools are enhancing the employee experience.

4. Adoption Metrics

Track the adoption rate of AI tools within the organisation:

1. **Several HR Staff Using AI Tools:**
   - o **Action:** Monitor the number of HR professionals actively using AI tools.
   - o **Impact:** Indicates the level of AI integration within the HR department.
2. **Frequency of Use:**

- o **Action:** Measure how often AI tools are used in daily HR workflows.
  - o **Impact:** Reflects the dependency on and trust in AI systems.
3. **Extent of Integration:**
   - o **Action:** Assess how deeply AI tools are integrated into HR processes.
   - o **Impact:** Shows the overall adoption and reliance on AI technologies.

Methods for Monitoring AI Systems

5. Regular Audits

Conduct regular audits to ensure AI systems are functioning correctly:

1. **Bias and Fairness Checks:**
   - o **Action:** Regularly audit AI algorithms to detect and correct biases.
   - o **Impact:** Ensures fairness and equity in AI-driven decisions.
2. **Data Integrity Verification:**
   - o **Action:** Periodically review data inputs to ensure they are accurate and relevant.
   - o **Impact:** Maintains the quality and reliability of AI outputs.
3. **Compliance Assessments:**
   - o **Action:** Ensure AI systems comply with evolving regulations and ethical guidelines.
   - o **Impact:** Prevents legal issues and promotes ethical AI use.

6. Continuous Feedback Loops

Implement continuous feedback mechanisms for ongoing improvement:

1. **User Reporting System:**
   - o **Action:** Allow users to report issues, provide suggestions, and share experiences with AI tools.

- o **Impact:** Facilitates real-time feedback and continuous enhancement.
2. **Feedback Analysis:**
   - o **Action:** Regularly analyse user feedback to identify common issues and areas for improvement.
   - o **Impact:** Drives iterative improvements based on user input.

7. Performance Dashboards

Utilise dashboards to provide real-time insights into AI performance:

1. **Real-Time Metrics Display:**
   - o **Action:** Create dashboards that show key performance indicators.
   - o **Impact:** Provides instant visibility into AI system performance.
2. **Highlight Areas Needing Attention:**
   - o **Action:** Use dashboards to identify and prioritise issues requiring immediate action.
   - o **Impact:** Ensures timely responses to potential problems.

8. Benchmarking

Compare AI performance against industry standards:

1. **Industry Surveys and Studies:**
   - o **Action:** Participate in surveys and studies to benchmark AI system performance.
   - o **Impact:** Identifies areas for improvement relative to industry peers.
2. **Set Improvement Targets:**
   - o **Action:** Use benchmarking data to set targets for performance enhancement.
   - o **Impact:** Ensures continuous progress and competitiveness.

Ensuring Continuous Improvement

9. Iterative Development

Treat AI implementation as an iterative process:

1. **Regular Updates:**
   - **Action:** Continuously refine AI models based on performance data and user feedback.
   - **Impact:** Keeps AI systems relevant and effective.
2. **Incorporate Best Practices:**
   - **Action:** Integrate the latest HR best practices into AI models.
   - **Impact:** Enhances the applicability and usefulness of AI tools.

10. Training and Support

Provide ongoing training and support for HR staff:

1. **Regular Training Sessions:**
   - **Action:** Offer periodic training to update HR staff on AI capabilities.
   - **Impact:** Ensures effective use of AI tools.
2. **Updated User Manuals:**
   - **Action:** Maintain up-to-date documentation and guides.
   - **Impact:** Provides continuous support and reference material.

11. Scalability and Flexibility

Ensure AI systems are scalable and flexible:

1. **Algorithm Updates:**
   - **Action:** Regularly update algorithms to incorporate new data and functionalities.
   - **Impact:** Maintains system performance and relevance.
2. **Expand Data Sets:**
   - **Action:** Continuously add new data to improve AI models.
   - **Impact:** Enhances accuracy and adaptability.

12. Ethical Considerations

Continuously evaluate the ethical implications of AI use in HR:

1. **Ethical Audits:**
    - o **Action:** Conduct regular audits to ensure AI systems adhere to ethical guidelines.
    - o **Impact:** Promotes fairness and transparency.
2. **Update Ethical Guidelines:**
    - o **Action:** Regularly revise ethical guidelines to address new challenges.
    - o **Impact:** Ensures ongoing ethical compliance.

Continuous monitoring and evaluation ensure AI systems remain effective and aligned with organisational goals. By implementing these practices, organisations can foster a culture of constant improvement and innovation.

The final chapter will provide a comprehensive AI integration plan, outlining the steps for a successful AI journey in HR. Join us as we chart the path forward and explore the future possibilities of AI in HR.

18. Charting the Path Forward: A Comprehensive AI Integration Plan

A Step-by-Step Guide to Effective AI Integration in HR

This concluding chapter summarises the key points covered in the book and provides a clear, step-by-step plan of action for integrating AI into HR functions. Each step includes checks and evaluation criteria to ensure successful implementation and guidance on when to move forward.

Step 1: Assess Needs and Opportunities

Summary

You can begin by identifying areas within HR where AI can add the most value. This includes recruitment, employee engagement, performance evaluation, and training.

Actions

1. **Conduct a Skills Audit:**

   - o **Action:** Evaluate current HR processes to identify inefficiencies.

   - o **Check:** Determine specific areas where AI can have an immediate impact.

   - o **Evaluation:** Move forward if clear opportunities for improvement are identified.

2. **Gather Team Input:**

   - o **Action:** Consult with HR team members to gather insights and suggestions.

   - o **Check:** Ensure diverse perspectives are considered.

   - o **Evaluation:** Proceed if there is consensus on potential AI use cases.

Step 2: Define Objectives and Develop a Strategy

Summary

Could you set clear, measurable objectives for your AI projects and develop a strategy aligning with your business goals? Yes, You can!

Actions

1. **Set SMART Goals:**

   o **Action:** Define Specific, Measurable, Achievable, Relevant, and Time-bound objectives.

   o **Check:** Ensure goals are realistic and align with business priorities.

   o **Evaluation:** Advance if goals are well-defined and agreed upon by stakeholders.

2. **Develop an AI Strategy:**

   o **Action:** Create a detailed strategy outlining how AI will be implemented.

   o **Check:** Include timelines, resource allocation, and critical milestones.

   o **Evaluation:** Move forward if the strategy is comprehensive and feasible.

Step 3: Pilot Testing and Incremental Implementation

Summary

Start with small-scale pilot projects to test AI applications in a controlled environment before full-scale deployment.

Actions

1. **Select Pilot Projects:**

- o **Action:** Choose specific HR functions for initial AI deployment.

- o **Check:** Ensure these functions have clear, measurable outcomes.

- o **Evaluation:** Proceed if pilot projects are well-defined and manageable.

2. **Implement and Test:**

- o **Action:** Deploy AI in selected areas and gather initial feedback.

- o **Check:** Monitor performance and address any issues.

- o **Evaluation:** Move to full implementation if pilot results are positive.

Step 4: Full-Scale Implementation and Training

Summary

Expand AI deployment across HR functions and provide comprehensive training to ensure the effective use of AI tools.

Actions

1. **Scale Up Deployment:**

- o **Action:** Roll out AI solutions across all relevant HR processes.

- o **Check:** Ensure scalability and integration with existing systems.

- o **Evaluation:** Proceed if AI tools perform well in the expanded scope.

2. **Conduct Training Programs:**

- o **Action:** Offer training sessions for HR staff on using AI tools.

- o **Check:** Ensure all users are comfortable and proficient with new technologies.

- o **Evaluation:** Move forward if training is successful and staff are confident using AI.

Step 5: Continuous Monitoring and Improvement

Summary

Regularly monitor AI systems to ensure they remain effective, fair, and aligned with organisational goals. Please continue to seek feedback and make necessary adjustments.

Actions

1. **Establish KPIs:**

   - o **Action:** Define key performance indicators to measure AI impact.

   - o **Check:** Ensure metrics cover efficiency, effectiveness, and user satisfaction.

   - o **Evaluation:** Proceed if KPIs show positive trends and improvements.

2. **Regular Audits and Feedback:**

   - o **Action:** Conduct regular audits and gather continuous feedback from users.

   - o **Check:** Identify areas for improvement and update AI systems accordingly.

   - o **Evaluation:** Move forward if AI systems consistently meet performance standards.

Step 6: Ethical Considerations and Compliance

Summary

Ensure that AI deployment adheres to ethical guidelines and complies with relevant regulations.

Actions

1. **Implement Ethical Guidelines:**

   - **Action:** Develop and enforce ethical AI use policies.

   - **Check:** Ensure guidelines are clear and regularly updated.

   - **Evaluation:** Proceed if ethical considerations are fully integrated into AI practices.

2. **Ensure Regulatory Compliance:**

   - **Action:** Regularly review AI systems for compliance with data privacy and other regulations.

   - **Check:** Conduct audits to ensure ongoing compliance.

   - **Evaluation:** If AI systems comply with all relevant laws and regulations, move forward.

Step 7: Foster a Culture of Innovation

Summary

Encourage an adaptive and innovative mindset within the HR team to continuously leverage AI advancements.

Actions

1. **Promote Continuous Learning:**

   - **Action:** Provide resources and opportunities for ongoing AI education.

- o **Check:** Encourage participation in AI-related training and events.

- o **Evaluation:** Proceed if the HR team actively engages in continuous learning.

2. **Encourage Experimentation:**

- o **Action:** Support trying new approaches and learning from failures.

- o **Check:** Recognize and reward innovative uses of AI.

- o **Evaluation:** Move forward if there is a culture of experimentation and learning.

By following this comprehensive AI integration plan, organisations can navigate the complexities of AI implementation and ensure a successful journey in HR. This approach will help unlock AI's full potential, driving innovation and enhancing HR's strategic value. Thank you for joining us on this journey.

The future of HR is here, and with the right approach, we can create more efficient, inclusive, and fulfilling workplaces. Let's embrace the possibilities and shape the future together.

Epilogue

As we conclude this journey through AI's transformative potential in HR, it's clear that the future of work is not just about technology but the harmonious integration of human and artificial intelligence. Throughout this book, we've explored how AI can revolutionise HR—from automating repetitive tasks and enhancing decision-making to creating more inclusive and fair workplaces.

But our journey does not end here. Integrating AI into HR is an ongoing process that requires continuous learning, adaptation, and vigilance. Our strategies, policies, and ethical considerations must evolve as AI technologies evolve. The road ahead will undoubtedly present new challenges, but it will also offer new opportunities for innovation and growth.

Reflecting on the insights and strategies presented in this book, a few key themes emerge:

Empathy and Ethics: AI can enhance HR processes but cannot replace the empathy and ethical judgment core to human interactions. As we leverage AI, we must ensure that our use of technology reflects our commitment to fairness, transparency, and respect for individual rights.

Continuous Improvement: Deploying AI is not a one-time event but a constant journey. Regular audits, feedback loops, and iterative improvements are essential to maintaining AI systems' effectiveness, fairness, and alignment with organisational goals.

Collaboration and Education: Successful AI integration requires collaboration across departments and continuous education for HR professionals. Building strong partnerships with IT, data science teams, and external experts will be crucial in navigating the complexities of AI.

Building Trust: Trust is the foundation of any successful AI implementation. We can build trust with employees and stakeholders by being transparent about AI's capabilities and limitations, involving stakeholders early, and maintaining human oversight.

Future Readiness: Preparing for the future means being agile and adaptable. As regulations evolve and new AI technologies emerge, staying informed and proactive will be vital in leveraging AI's full potential.

AI's potential to reshape HR is immense as we look to the future. However, it is up to us to ensure that this transformation benefits everyone. By embracing ethical principles, fostering a culture of continuous learning, and maintaining a human-centric approach, we can create workplaces that are not only more efficient but also more humane.

Thank you for joining us on this journey. May the insights and strategies shared in this book inspire you to explore new possibilities, drive positive change, and lead your organisation into a bright and innovative future.

With optimism and commitment,

Chirag Kansara (chirag@appliview.com)

www.ingramcontent.com/pod-product-compliance
Lightning Source LLC
Chambersburg PA
CBHW041335120726
48005CB00014B/2269